Ricky Ohl

Software for e-Consultation Corpus Analysis and Representation

GRIN Verlag

Bibliografische Information der Deutschen Nationalbibliothek:

Die Deutsche Bibliothek verzeichnet diese Publikation in der Deutschen National-
bibliografie; detaillierte bibliografische Daten sind im Internet über http://dnb.d-
nb.de/ abrufbar.

Imprint:

Copyright © 2011 GRIN Verlag GmbH
Druck und Bindung: Books on Demand GmbH, Norderstedt Germany
ISBN: 978-3-656-01256-6

This book at GRIN:

http://www.grin.com/en/e-book/179025/software-for-e-consultation-corpus-analysis-
and-representation

GRIN - Your knowledge has value

Der GRIN Verlag publiziert seit 1998 wissenschaftliche Arbeiten von Studenten, Hochschullehrern und anderen Akademikern als eBook und gedrucktes Buch. Die Verlagswebsite www.grin.com ist die ideale Plattform zur Veröffentlichung von Hausarbeiten, Abschlussarbeiten, wissenschaftlichen Aufsätzen, Dissertationen und Fachbüchern.

Visit us on the internet:

http://www.grin.com/

http://www.facebook.com/grincom

http://www.twitter.com/grin_com

The name(s) of the author(s)

Dr. Ricky Ohl

Title

Software for e-Consultation Corpus Analysis and Representation.

The affiliation(s) and address(es) of the author(s)

SAE / Qantm College, Senior Lecturer in Games Programming

Abstract

The global phenomenon of electronic(e)-governance and the advanced capacity for information generation by information and communication technologies (ICTs) have contributed to the perceived problem of information overload. In participatory democracy and specifically e-democracy and e-consultation, in which a vast quantity and array of textual discourse can be generated, effective and efficient information processing is important. Effective and efficient processing will assist participants to make-sense of and remain engaged in consultations. Accordingly, tools and technologies to assist in the analysis, synthesis and dissemination of such discourse have the potential to make a salient contribution. In this article, a critique of several software packages, consisting of qualitative text analysis, natural language text mining and computer supported argument visualisation software is presented. The use of natural language text mining software with sentiment analysis features was the initial focus of this investigation. However, early in the investigation and after a software trial, natural language text mining software was considered underdeveloped with regard to the specific functionality sought. Hence, the investigation then focused primarily on the utility of computer supported argument visualisation (CSAV) and also text analysis software. For text analysis, Leximancer, Text Analyst Atlas.ti. and TextSTAT were preferred and chosen from among eleven programmes investigated. For CSAV software, a programme called Compendium was preferred and chosen from among twelve programmes investigated.

Keywords

Computer Supported Argument Visualisation, Knowledge Cartography, Qualitative Text Analysis, e-Democracy, e-Consultation, Natural Language Text Mining, Wicked Problems

TABLE OF CONTENTS

Software for e-Consultation Corpus Analysis and Representation.

Abstract

The global phenomenon of electronic(e)-governance and the advanced capacity for information generation by information and communication technologies (ICTs) have contributed to the perceived problem of information overload. In participatory democracy and specifically e-democracy and e-consultation, in which a vast quantity and array of textual discourse can be generated, effective and efficient information processing is important. Effective and efficient processing will assist participants to make-sense of and remain engaged in consultations. Accordingly, tools and technologies to assist in the analysis, synthesis and dissemination of such discourse have the potential to make a salient contribution. In this article, a critique of several software packages, consisting of qualitative text analysis, natural language text mining and computer supported argument visualisation software is presented. The use of natural language text mining software with sentiment analysis features was the initial focus of this investigation. However, early in the investigation and after a software trial, natural language text mining software was considered underdeveloped with regard to the specific functionality sought. Hence, the investigation then focused primarily on the utility of computer supported argument visualisation (CSAV) and also text analysis software. For text analysis, Leximancer, Text Analyst Atlas.ti. and TextSTAT were preferred and chosen from among eleven programmes investigated. For CSAV software, a programme called Compendium was preferred and chosen from among twelve programmes investigated.

e-Democracy and e-Consultation

The proliferation of ICTs and the impact of the Internet has led to a global phenomenon where increasingly corporate and public institutions are moving to conduct administration and the delivery services and programmes online (Rathee and Rishi 2011). An overarching term for this phenomenon is electronic(e) governance, but the element in which governments engage with citizens on democratic matters, enabled via the use of ICTs and the Internet is known as e-democracy (OECD 2003). E-democracy can be partitioned into two distinct categories, 1) electronic voting, and relevant to this research 2) electronic participation, which provides greater opportunity for civic engagement and citizen consultation in public policy-making (Macintosh 2004). One of the mechanisms being utilised for such participatory democracy is e-consultation. In e-consultation, elected representatives and government agencies use ICTs and the Internet to consult the citizenry on matters of democratic governance. For the purposes of this research, a case study was conducted on a significant public consultation programme in Queensland, Australia. The consultation was initiated by the Queensland State Government for the development of the South-East Queensland (SEQ) Regional Plan. In this case, a draft SEQ Regional Plan was released to the public for feedback. Several mechanisms were used to engage participants, including town meetings, postal and electronic public submissions and an online forum or e-Consultation. This study was scoped to focus on the e-Consultation component of the programme.

Participatory Planning

Such participatory planning processes and consultations around regional, urban and town planning evoke critical questions. How can diverse perspectives from the citizenry, different community groups, planners, and government, consultation discourse and decision rationale be captured, analysed, synthesised and represented? How can the government and public stakeholders of regional planning consultations make sense of such a high volume and diverse discourse? (De Liddo and Buckingham Shum 2007). The high volume and complexity of information generated in consultative democracy can make it difficult for both the public and government to assimilate.

ICTs, Information Overload and Information Processing

The advanced information processing and networked capabilities of ICTs, has led to a state where information overload is a regularly cited problem (Ficco and Karamychev 2004; Baez et al. 2010). Accordingly, information processing and sense-making is of particular relevance in the burgeoning field of e-Democracy and consultative forums, which have the potential to generate large quantities of data and requires accurate and efficient analysis of discourse. Although being a contributor of the overload issue, ICTs may also be part of the solution (Eppler and Mengis 2004). Toward these ends, the Organisation for Economic Co-operation and Development (OECD) posed the question of whether technology can adequately support the analysis and summarisation of democracy consultation text submissions (OECD 2004). Furthermore, Coleman and Norris (2005), and Renton and Macintosh (2004) found that there is a need for research that looks at tools and technologies that can aid in the analysis, synthesis and dissemination of participatory democracy discourse.

CSAV

Computer supported argument visualisation (CSAV) has been found particularly applicable to support the analysis and representation of complex data such as those in consultative design activities in regional, urban and town planning (Conklin et al. 2007; Kirschner et al. 2003; Swedish Morphological Society 2005; Rittel and Webber 1984). This medium can help establish common ground within diversity, understand positions, surface assumptions and collectively construct consensus (Kirshchner et al. 2003). Within this environment, CSAV can therefore function to deliver an enhanced level of democratic transparency.

Software Application

A proposition from the E-democracy European Network project was that natural language processing is likely to be an effective tool for analysis, sorting and classifying communications (Carenini et al. 2007; Whyte and Macintosh 2003). Manual discourse analysis can be a time consuming and expensive undertaking and as participation in public consultation increases, this exercise is likely to become more burdensome. The e-Democracy Unit of the Queensland Government supported this fact. If an organisation does not have the means to analyse communications in an efficient and effective manner, this deficiency can contribute to misinterpretation and misappropriation of communications (Bontis et al. 2003). Both quantitative and qualitative methods of content analysis are needed to aid in making sense of the myriad of voices in public consultations and enable representatives to summarise and explain the deliberative process (Whyte and Macintosh 2003).

Text Mining Software in e-Consultation

An obvious advantage of e-Consultation over face-to-face consultation is that the discussion threads are stored and available for qualitative and quantitative analysis (Whyte and Macintosh 2003). Furthermore, consultation forum text of participant discourse is in the participant's own words as opposed to being paraphrased by a facilitator, which may contribute to a more trustworthy process (Whyte and Macintosh 2003). Thread analysis is a useful feature of an electronic-forum data analysis process, which is used for the analysis of e-consultations in urban planning (Jankowski et al. 1997). Thread analysis can provide both quantitative and qualitative data to aid in assessing, which topics, issues or questions stimulated participants and the extent that particular topics attracted in-depth discussion. The assessment measures can include, quantity of comments posted per thread, the average and total word count per thread and thread depth (i.e. amount of levels of reply, and length of time between first and last contribution) (Whyte and Macintosh 2003).

Qualitative Text Analysis Software

Weitzman (Weitzman 2003) argues that debate regarding opposition to researchers' use of qualitative data analysis software (QDAS) is based around the perception that software will do the analysis for the researcher or analyst. A counter-argument, which is well supported in the literature, is that it is the researchers' responsibility to understand his /her chosen research approach and thus, effectively guide and interpret the analysis (Gilbert 2002; Macmillan and Koenig 2004; Morse and Richards 2002; Weitzman 2003; Atherton and Elsmore 2007). Furthermore, Weitzman (2003) argues that analysis software is only a support tool in theory building. Table 1 lists a number of reasons that have been cited for the beneficial use of QDAS.

Table 1 – Benefits of QDAS	
Benefit	Citations
To facilitate data management	(Blismas and Dainty 2003; Welsh 2002)
Search facilities	(Blismas and Dainty 2003)
Greater methodological transparency	(Bringer et al. 2004; Dainty et al. 2000)
To alleviate the time consuming aspects of qualitative research	(Dainty et al. 2000)
useful for developing the themes and their relationships	(Bringer et al. 2004)
Consolidation of all data and theory in the one place supports the analysis process	(Weitzman 2003)
Consistency helps the researcher to undertake careful exploration of the data	(Weitzman 2003)
Speed allows the researcher to undertake greater exploration of the data	(Weitzman 2003)
Representation helps the researcher to visualise and extend their thinking of the data and therefore assist in theory building	(Weitzman 2003)
Free up time formally spent in data management and encoding, enabling richer data evaluation.	(Mangabeira et al. 2004)
Most adapted from: Soliman and Kan (2004, p. 2)	

Software Functionality Sought

The ideal functionality for the technology that was sought for the project was: (1) semi-automated analysis; (2) qualitative natural language text mining and analysis, along with (3) quantitative features to enable enhanced data description. Functionality was sought that would enable (3a) filtering, (3b) classifying and (3c) synthesis of each participant's text posting. The technology was to be used to (4) draw out the major concepts from the dialogue text and (5) visually map their interrelationships. Technical functionality was also sought that would enable the (6) highlighting of areas of agreement and disagreement and

(7) investigating participant sentiment. Various off-the-shelf software packages provided some of the features sought but no one package provided all of them.

The term text mining refers to a technology that functions to automatically discover patterns and trends in large collections of unstructured text (Uramoto et al. 2004). Text mining functions to assist the organisation and visualisation of text in multiple ways either at the document or text level. These technologies use algorithms to analyse the text from user specified perspectives. Examples of these perspectives are, associations and trends between entity categories such as between researcher names and research topics; medical drugs, drug effects and disease symptoms; consultation participants and discourse topics (Mack et al. 2004).

Software Investigated

The text mining software packages with automation trialled were, Logik (Coredge Software Inc. 2003), Copernic Summariser (Copernic Inc. 2001), AnSWR (Centers for Disease Control and Prevention 2003), CATPAC (Woelfel 1998), TextAnalyst (MicroSystems Co. Ltd. 2003) and Leximancer (McFadden 2003). DB2 Information Integrator OmniFind Edition (IBM 2004), Microsoft Excel, Nvivo (QSR International Pty Ltd 2002) and Atlas.ti (Muhr 2004) were the manual text analysis applications trialled. In addition, a quantitative text analysis software trialled was TextStat (Huning 2007). The CSAV software trialled included Compendium (Bachler et al. 2007), Reason!able (Van Gelder and Bulka 2002), Mind Manager (Mindjet LLC 2007) and Decision Explorer (Banxia Software Ltd 2004). All of the software packages presented in this discussion, can be run in a Microsoft Windows environment on a personal computer.

Semi-Automated Text Mining Software

Logik is a commercial knowledge discovery tool that helps users to access knowledge from within unstructured electronic information. It exposes document content in the form of summaries and key themes from electronic information such as e-mail, files in public folders or local hard drives and documents on the Internet. It enables users to define algorithms for a specific search focus but its features specialise in document search rather than text analysis, which was the focus of this project (Coredge Software Inc. 2003).

Copernic Summariser is a commercial automated text summariser that extracts concepts from inputted documents to provide a document summary or overview. The program processes text using semantic analysers and statistical models attaching a weighting to sentences and displays a summary of content based on its relative importance. Although a useful tool, it does not enable the user control over the analysis process, which was desired for this project (Copernic Inc. 2001).

AnSWR derived from 'Analysis Software for Word-Based Records' is a free public domain tool originally developed to assist with managing and analysing large multi-site research studies that integrate qualitative and quantitative techniques. It enables analysts to analyse unstructured or semi-structured textual data, explain how analytical decisions evolved and to examine the validity of the analytical lens used to frame, filter and present information. Features are included for coding and indexing of ideas or themes, ordering codes, and establishing relationships between codes. Text retrieval is aided by the ability to select sub-sets of information using search parameters such as files, codes, coders, segments and attributes of information sources. It provides an *audit trail* that is useful for explaining how concepts, theories and propositions were developed (Centers for Disease Control and Prevention 2003).

CATPAC is a commercial intelligent program that can read text and summarise its main ideas. CATPAC is fully automated and thus, needs no precoding and makes no linguistic assumptions. Catpac also provides a variety of neural network options and cluster analysis algorithms. A case delimiter can be inserted at the end of each respondent's text dialogue, thus the program will then treat each delimited text section as a separate case. It was not designed to include a wide range of known text analysis methods but positioned to fill a market niche, which was fully automatic analysis of text without extensive pre coding, independent of any linguistic theory or heuristics. Once again, user control over the text analysis process is limited (Woelfel 1998).

TextAnalyst is a commercial text analysis program that is capable of semi-automated natural language text analysis from arbitrary fields. It processes text, develops and displays clusters and semantic relationships between words and topics within the text. The software analysis displays results by significance, as hyperlinked words that can be clicked to access and view corresponding text sections. This enables efficient navigation of large texts and for comparison within and between texts. The software creates automatic summaries of texts and the text base can be queried for information retrieval using natural language queries (MicroSystems Co. Ltd. 2003). The figure below is an example of the output from an analysis of the SEQ Regional Plan Consultation discourse corpus using TextAnalyst.

Text Analyst Output Example

Figure 1 – TextAnalyst Output

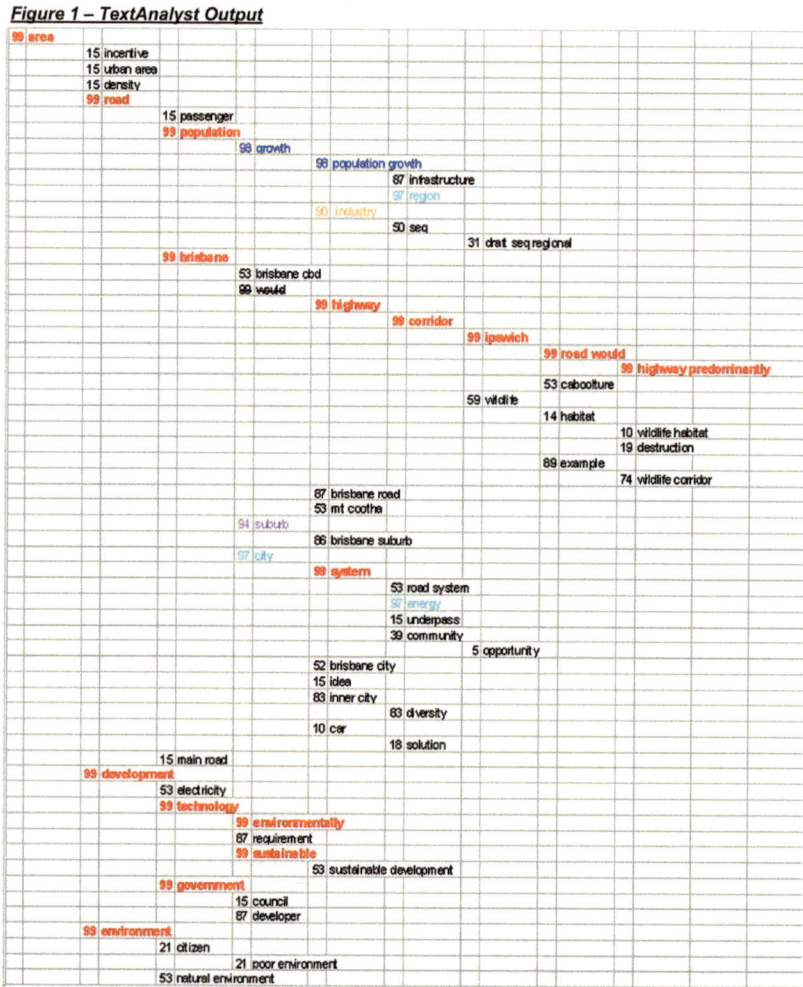

Leximancer is a commercial data-mining tool used for analysing the content of textual documents and displaying the elicited concepts and their interrelationships visually in a clustered map of concepts. It enables the efficient analysis of vast amounts of text. Concepts within a text are displayed in a manner that enables further exploration of their related subtext (Smith 2004a; Smith and Humpreys 2006). Leximancer provides the following sources of information about the content of textual documents.

1. *"The main concepts contained with the text and their relative importance*
2. *The strengths between concepts (how often they co-occur)*
3. *The centrality of each concept*
4. *The similarities in the context in which they occur"* (Smith 2004b, pp. 4 & 8).

The prominence of concepts is displayed visually, by colours and colour intensity (i.e. the brighter the colour the more prominent a word). The size of the boundary circles around words also denotes prominence and their relational sphere with other words. Leximancer provides for inter-textual comparative analysis and was used in this project to identify significant categories, which were then used to inform the grounded theory coding process.

Leximancer Analysis Examples

The two figures below show the output of the processing of public submissions from the SEQ Regional Plan Consultation by Leximancer. The text analysis represented by these examples shows the online submissions only because this information is publicly assessable and therefore public knowledge. However, the identification of patterns and themes was informed by the analysis of all SEQ Regional Plan Consultation submissions and not only what is displayed here.

Figure 2 - Leximancer Output

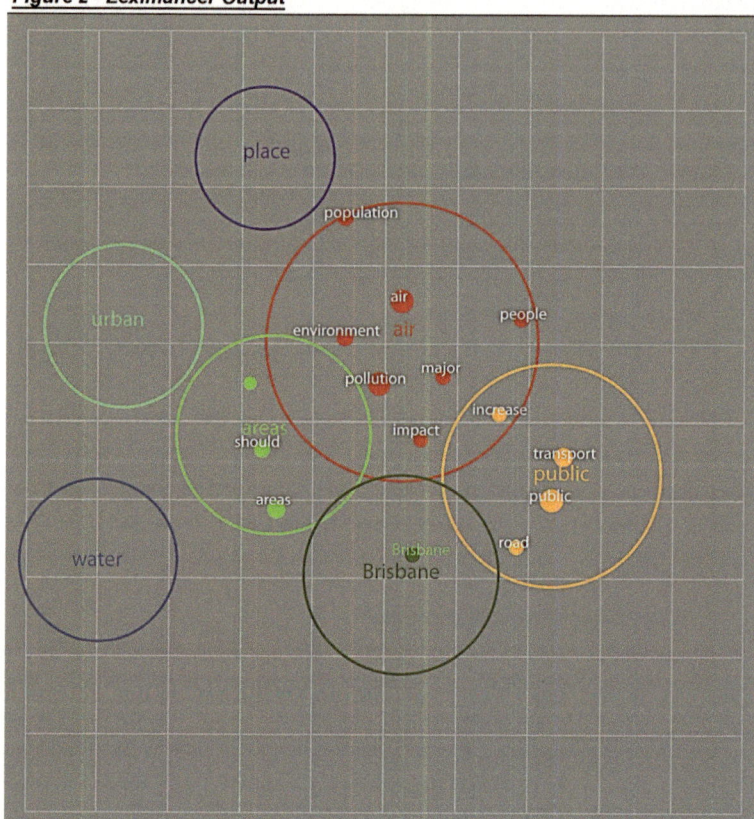

Figure 3 shows the concepts elicited from the SEQ Regional Plan e-Consultation discourse text and when using the software, each of these concepts can be clicked on to access their associated full text.

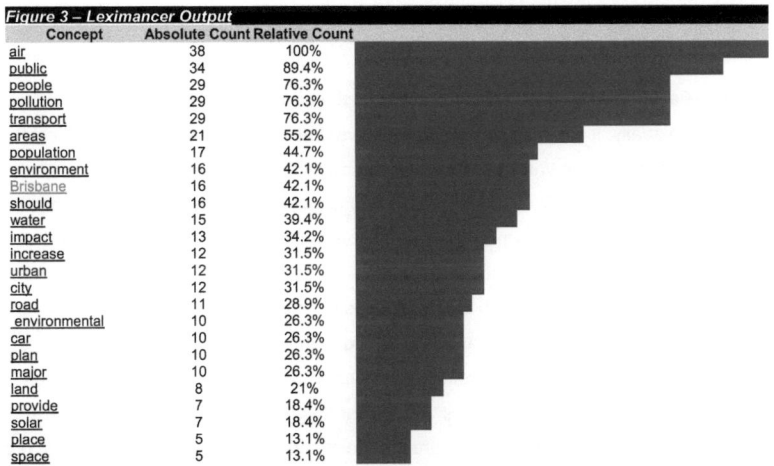

Figure 3 – Leximancer Output

Concept	Absolute Count	Relative Count
air	38	100%
public	34	89.4%
people	29	76.3%
pollution	29	76.3%
transport	29	76.3%
areas	21	55.2%
population	17	44.7%
environment	16	42.1%
Brisbane	16	42.1%
should	16	42.1%
water	15	39.4%
impact	13	34.2%
increase	12	31.5%
urban	12	31.5%
city	12	31.5%
road	11	28.9%
environmental	10	26.3%
car	10	26.3%
plan	10	26.3%
major	10	26.3%
land	8	21%
provide	7	18.4%
solar	7	18.4%
place	5	13.1%
space	5	13.1%

Manual Text Analysis Software

In 2004, IBM was regarded by Gartner Research as the industry leader and most visionary developers of unstructured natural language text analysis software (Shegda et al. 2004). IBM's related research and development includes text mining, sentiment analysis and/or sincerity metrics. Their leadership in these areas continues in 2011 (Fouts and Rozwell 2011; Adrian and Genovese 2011). Hence, text mining software from IBM software, DB2 Information Integrator OmniFind Edition was obtained for trial in this project.

IBM DB2® Information Integrator OmniFind Edition is commercial text mining software designed for searching enterprise-wide structured and unstructured information repositories. IBM's research and development had been conducting research on the design of an add-in sentiment analysis component for IBM DB2® Information Integrator OmniFind Edition® (Yi, Nasukawa, Bunescu and Niblack, 2003). The objective of sentiment analysis is to identify how writers' sentiments are expressed in texts and whether these indicate favourable or unfavourable opinions toward a subject of inquiry (Nasukawa and Yi 2003). Obviously, citizen sentiment toward policy issues is of significance in democracy.

To accommodate the technical specifications of this application, specifications were a computer with 64 bit CPU, running Linux operating system and 4 gigabits of RAM. However, after a trial of the computer and software, it was found that this category of technology had been stuck in the search engine phase and thus was not as advanced as was hoped and therefore was not used in this project.

NVivo is a commercial product that enables sophisticated qualitative analysis of digital text data contextually. It can also provide quantitative data on word tokens (i.e. an object that has a text attribute, the value of which is a computational string), word count and percentage occurrence of words or word tokens. NVivo is designed to allow a focus on language via the analysis of text unit relations not only at a micro-level (i.e. per line or word) which is common in available software but also at the macro-level (i.e. sentence or paragraph). Accordingly, it enables text mining for particular words, phases or collocations using text-string searches and text-pattern searches. Text-string searching refers to simple word and phrase searches. Whereas, text-pattern searching refers to the performance of queries in order to search for text for repetition, variant word forms with similar rhyme schemes or recurrent phrases (Durian, 2002). These are useful features for deciphering "*symbolic or metaphorical relations between spans of text or for discovering trends within the data*" (Durian 2002, p. 739).

Additional features in NVivo that were relevant to this grounded case study research were; NVivo enables users to annotate memos about text (i.e. memoing), users can dissect a text into user-defined sections to perform comparative analysis of sections visually. In addition, users can export node diagrams from NVivo into concept mapping programs and manipulate connections (Durian 2002).

Atlas.ti is a commercial qualitative analysis programme that provides functionality to manually process large bodies of textual, graphical, audio and video data. It offers features to enable systematic quoting, coding of data and memoing (Muhr 2004). Codes can take the form of either user customised or in-vivo codes and be applied to user specified data sections (i.e. delimited). User annotations can be assigned to each of the data segments, codes and memos. Atlas.ti provides functionality for a limited form of mind mapping and graphical network editing (See Figure 4). The generation to html format for publishing to the Internet is also a feature, which provides an additional option for sharing analyses. This software provides features for a systematic approach to data analysis but it is not prescriptive (i.e. freeform application). This means that there is minimal data preparation required and its application is less formalised enabling greater flexibility than some other qualitative analysis packages. See examples of data analysis in figures 4 and 5.

Atlas.ti Analysis Examples

Figure 4 – Atlas.ti Graphical Semantic Network

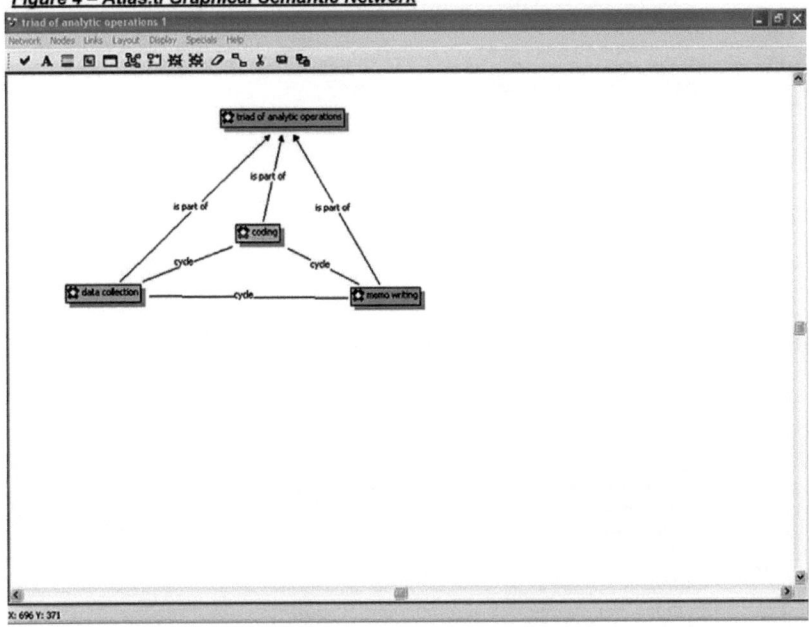

Figure 5 – Atlas.ti Analysis Output

001 **e-Consultation Population**
002 **802 participants**
003 **1925 postings**
004
005 **Caring for the place we call home: The Draft
   Regional Plan limits development in certain
   areas of South East Queensland to prevent our
   towns and cities spreading out too far. This
   protects our forests, regional landscape,
   farmlands, coastline and waterways.**
006
007 **1. Do you think these assets are an important
   part of SEQ and need to be protected?**
008
009 Agree (431 / 92.688%) Disagree (34 / 7.311%)   ⬜ ✿ Pro ✿ Con
010 **Total** = 465
011
012 **Caring for the place we call home:**
013
014 **2. If you disagree, what do you think is the
   most important attribute of SEQ that must be
   protected?**
015
016 287 117 Ecologically sustainable developments   ✿ Argument
   and the decision making being made at the local   ✿ Eco Friendly Development
   council level.   ✿ Local Gov Decisions
017
018 367 153 This does not concern just people, but
   more importantly wildlife, whose habitat we are
   taking and we have to live in harmony, not destroy
   them. Ultimately the land clearing for human   ✿ Answer
   development will destroy the very reason people   ✿ Argument
   come here and it will also change the weather. I   ✿ Climate change
   have contacted the Council and Government   ✿ Land Clearing
   many times on this issue, and while giving all the
   reasons that they have it in hand, the bulldozers
   continue to work daily destroying the wildlife
   habitat. For money, power and greed, humans are
   destroying themselves. There is also the issue of
   Karma.
019
020 417 181 Current flora and fauna, clean air, clean   ✿ Answer
   water supply, and public health and safety. SEQ   ✿ Argument
   has important koala habitat that is under threat   ✿ Clean Air
   from development. Water is also at a premium as
   population numbers increase. Public health and
   safety requires good social infrastructure that
   facilitates caring and concerned communities
   where people feel that they belong and have
   friends.
021
022 1283 529 Air quality, water quality, biodiversity, ✿ Answer
   minimal greenhouse emissions, minimal use of   ✿ Argument

TextSTAT is a free simple quantitative text analysis programme. It can read multiple text and html files to produce word frequency lists and concordances. TextSTAT enables the user to search text corpuses to find the frequency of particular words and word forms. A word form example is, a search on the word *road* produced: road, roads, road-rage, road-conditions, unroadworthy, roadside, on-road, main road and roadways. TextSTAT also contains a technical feature named a *spider*, which enables searches of multiple web pages from a particular website (Huning 2007). In this project, TextSTAT was used to investigate the common vernacular in the SEQ Regional Plan Consultation discourse. The purpose of this activity was to investigate the usability of the argument ontology grammar and notation used in the consultation maps.

Several qualitative text analysis and/or mining software, in addition to those discussed above were also trialled. These did not offer anything conceptually new nor of value beyond those already presented and therefore were not discussed. These consisted of **Apollo**, **Text Mining for Clementine**, **Intext**, **Inxight**, **SmartDiscovery**, **ISYS: desktop**, **MAXQDA**, **Tropes** and **Zoom**.

Text Analysis Software Preferences
The researcher's preferences from among the text analysis programmes trialled in this study were **Leximancer** for automated text processing because it processed a large volume of data efficiently, its output was informative and relatively easy to comprehend, and it offered multiple ways to view analyses and data drill-down functionality. Leximancer was very beneficial in the analysis process and was a good starting point to inform further manual qualitative analysis and the automated analysis is bias and politically neutral. Thus, automated analysis can also serve for comparison with manual analysis to enhance trustworthiness. In addition, **TextAnalyst** provided an analysis contrast for the Leximancer output. **Atlas ti** was the preferred tool for manual text analysis. It enabled greater flexibility in the analysis process with less data preparation and therefore was less constricting and more efficient than the other software trialled. Flexibility was relevant to the purpose of this research due to it being descriptive research and using a grounded theory method where concepts were emergent. However, in research where categories are more developed, a more structured analysis could be beneficial and in such cases NVivo might be a better choice. In fact, as far as backup service and support for the software is concerned, NVivo was much better supported by its developers. Lastly, **TextSTAT** effectively served the basic

functionality that was sought in this project for the quantitative analysis of text, which consisted of word frequencies only.

Submissions' Analysis Process & CSAV Mapping

All submissions to the SEQ Regional Plan Consultation were digitally collected and stored, enabling: computer aided sorting, coding, text mining, analysis and direct CSAV mapping. Keyword searches were performed to identify submission' content relevant to the specific subject area investigated (i.e. environmental atmosphere). The submissions' text was analysed using the three qualitative text analysis software applications mentioned, Leximancer, Text Analyst and Atlas.ti. In addition, TextSTAT was used for basic quantitative text analysis. This approach provided triangulation in the text analysis process. The analysis of submissions and the identification of patterns within this text informed the selection of themes to represent in maps and for the coding used in further detailed analysis and grounded theory development.

After processing with Leximancer and TextAnalyst, Atlas.ti was then used for finer detailed manual analysis of the textual discourse. This supported the identification of the **issues** [▮], **arguments** [✖], **questions** [▮], **answers** [▮], **pros** [➕] and **cons** [➖], and **notes** [▮] (i.e. non-specific additional comments) which were then represented in maps. **Decision** nodes [▲] (i.e. representing government decisions) and **reference** nodes [▮] (i.e. representing a link to additional or external reference materials), were used only in the analysis and mapping of the Government Reports' content in this study. **Map** nodes [▮] were used throughout maps as they enable hyper-linking between maps. **List** nodes [▮] (i.e. represents a list or container for other nodes) were not required by the map-maker in this specific case (see also Table 2). Furthermore, as well as categorising and labelling the discourse content by Compendium argument notation, this process enabled the identification of emergent themes from the text which also acted to consolidate many of the themes highlighted by the automated qualitative text analysis software.

Manual Search Terms Used

The search terms used to elicit appropriate textual content from the large corpus of consultation discourse were informed by the submissions' text analysis and were then used to search the government reports to find associated information within the reports that related to the themes within participants' submissions. The search terms and word forms consisted of **air** quality, **greenhouse** effect, **green house**, **population** growth, **climate** change, **development**, **solar** energy, **conservation**, renewable **energy**, **sea levels**, global **warming, land clearing.**

CSAV Software

Computer supported argument visualisation consists of a range of multimedia tools where computer software is used to analyse and graphically represent discourse and deliberation in diagrammatic form using nodes and link lines (Kirshchner et al. 2003). Several computer supported argument visualisation packages were investigated to determine the best fit for this project. These packages consisted of Decision Explorer (Banxia Software Ltd 2004), MindManager (Mindjet LLC 2007), Reason!able (Van Gelder and Bulka 2002), CmapTools (Institute for Human and Machine Cognition 2007), Araucaria (Reed and Rowe 2003), Belvedere (Suthers and Burger 2002) and Compendium (Bachler et al. 2007), Inspiration, ConceptDraw, MINDMAP, FreeMind, Athena Standard, and Athena Negotiator. The ideal CSAV software features that were considered applicable to the project environment were:

- Flexibility in argument visualisation or map layout.
- Ability to evaluate argumentation.
- An argument ontology and node notation that was powerful enough to deal with multifarious discourse but will not straightjacket the analysis.
- Text features to enable expressive representation of content.
- Graphical features (i.e. node shapes, import of graphics).
- A range of node linking features.
- Accommodation of external file types and from disparate programs.
- Ability to report argument or consultation discourse decisions.
- Multiple forms or publishing of visualisations.
- Features to enable coping with large quantities of data.
- Synchronous collaborative operation.
- Ability to weight argument nodes for qualitative analysis of arguments and may be applied as a form of participant voting.
- A value for money product.

CSAV Software Investigated

The Strategic Options Development and Analysis (Soda) method uses interviews and cognitive mapping to represent individuals' views on an issue (Eden 1992). The evolution of Soda, led to the development of software called COPE which is now commercially available as Banxia 'Decision Explorer' (Banxia Software Ltd. 2002). Soda does not offer formal node notation whereas the IBIS ontology in Compendium software does provide for node notation (see Compendium notation detail in Table 2).

	Table 2 – Compendium Node Types	
	Node Type	Description
?	Question Node	This represents a Question or Issue for discussion.
	Answer Node	The represents an Answer or Position, often in response to a question or issue.
	Map Node	This represents a map, which is a container for other nodes and links. This can be used to: - create a 'picture' of the relationships between ideas; - group questions and ideas together in meaningful clusters; - create associative links between nodes.
	List Node	This represents a list, which is a container for other nodes. List nodes can be used to create a sortable list of nodes, which will usually be a collection of nodes that do not need to be linked with each other (associative links).
+	Pro Node	This represents a response in favour of an answer or position.
—	Con Node	This represents a response against an answer or position.
	Reference Node	This represents a link to some additional, external reference material, which can be in the form of a web link or Word document etc. These nodes can also be linked to images, which will then be scaled and used instead of the usual reference node icon.
	Note Node	This represents some non-specific, additional comment or notation, often about a node or the current view.
	Decision Node	This represents a decision reached, usually from an answer or position about a question or issue.
	Argument Node	This represents a general argument, usually in response to an answer or position.
(Bachler et al. 2006)		

Table 2 displays the IBIS related link inferences and associated colours from Compendium.

Decision Explorer is a commercial idea-mapping tool designed to support the management of 'soft issues' or qualitative information surrounding complex or uncertain situations. The software enables users to represent detailed thoughts and ideas in order to gain insight through exploration and interpretation. Its features allow the user to capture and analyse ideas in order to explicate their interrelationships (Banxia Software Ltd. 2002). Banxia Software Ltd. (2002) proposes that the software can be utilised to represent themes and concepts elicited from research data. Decision explorer provides a free form mapping environment but does not provide an argument ontology.

The reasons this product was not chosen are: (1) Cost - Decision Explorer is a commercial product whereas Compendium (described below) is a free product with a very motivated and responsive development team. (2) Compendium has a vibrant research and practitioner community whereas Decision Explorer is not publicly accountable. (3) Decision Explorer also Soda focuses on small group facilitation whereas IBIS ontology within Compendium was designed with a large population in mind (i.e. urban planning).

MindManager is a commercial mapping tool that builds maps out from a central root topic with topic and sub-topic branches, creating what is referred to in this research as star, cluster and/or spider maps. It is a useful tool for mind mapping which is the purpose of its design. Nodes can be shaped as rectangles, circles, ovals, hexagons or underlines only (Mindjet LLC 2007). Text formatting is well developed but the importing and utilisation of external graphics has limitations and its map structuring is restrictive. Its development was not based on a specific argument ontology such as IBIS but these icons could be added to its software library. A very good feature of MindManager is its integration with Microsoft applications and the functionality to export map content to applications such as Microsoft Word in an indented text, or report layout.

Reason!able is a commercial argument mapping software based on a simplified version of Toulmin argumentation (Van Gelder and Bulka 2002). It constructs maps in a top-down hierarchy representing conclusions, objections and reasons. Map structure is automated in this fashion and thus prescriptive and inflexible. It provides for the manual evaluation of argumentation based on a Likert scale weighting for nodes which consists of, *conclusive, strong, weak* or *no support*. Its graphical range is limited, as is does not have the functionality to import external graphics and text formatting is restricted. However, this product performs well within its strictly defined functionality; that is, reasoning and argumentation in education and for the visual representation of reasoning and evidence for and against a statement of claim (van Gelder in Kirschner et al. 2003). bCisive is a current derivative of Reason!able and it includes IBIS grammar as an option for argument map nodes. This development further attests to the applicability of IBIS notation.

Cmap Tools is a free concept mapping software offering rectangular and circled nodes with labelled links (Institute for Human and Machine Cognition 2007). Map structure is freeform but top down structure can also be automated. It does not offer an argument ontology or node notation. Node, text and links can be formatted for additional expression. Link styles (e.g. dotted), shape (e.g. curve) and thickness are editable. This program also provides a spell check for map content. Overall, graphic expression is relatively basic. External reference materials can be attached to maps and maps can be published to the Internet and mapped collaboratively. The Internet collaboration feature is a very beneficial for collaborative mapping by users in dispersed locations.

Araucaria is free argument mapping and analysis software. It enables the importing of text into the working frame so that argument maps can be built from the text using a point and click process (Rowe, Reed & Katzav, 2003). Araucaria enables argument visualisation based on a simplified Toulmin scheme (Toulmin et al. 1984) and Wigmore diagramming (Wigmore 1931). Yet, schemes for the analysis of arguments are user customisable. Thus, it provides for the analysis of text in a customisable form. Its graphical expressiveness, text formatting and integration with disparate applications are restricted. Map or node notation is not provided and map structuring is automated and thus in the sense of this   project is restrictive.

Belvedere is a commercial collaborative evidence and concept mapping tool (Suthers and Burger 2002). It does not provide argument notation for nodes and its graphical expression is basic. Its ontology is loosely based on Toulmin's model of argumentation. This programme supports a structured argument approach (Suthers 2005). Thus, is not as flexible as programmes based on the IBIS ontology.

Compendium is a free, semantic argument visualisation tool, based on the IBIS ontology and grammar (Bachler et al. 2007). Horst Rittel's Issue Based Information System (IBIS) was specifically developed to aid in dealing with wicked problems in urban planning (Kunz and Rittel 1979). Compendium is typically used as a tool to support the real time mapping of discussions in meetings, collaborative modelling, and the longer-term management of this information as organisational memory. In the project, Compendium was used to visually represent concepts elicited from the SEQ Regional Plan Consultation discourse and SEQ Regional Plan policy.

Compendium has a very dynamic user population and research and development team. This is evidenced by a collaborative online Compendium community regularly discussing usage issues and reporting feature requests and bugs. Compendium has been developed in response to this collaboration resulting in 16 publicly released new versions from January 2003 to June 2011. Hence, the development a computer supported argument visualisation software, which is based on the IBIS ontology has occurred through intuitive practitioner and traditional notions. Buckingham Shum (2006a, pers. comm. 18 September), a researcher on the Compendium development team, reported that:

> "Compendium's development as a software and methodology project has been driven by user feedback, research interests (e.g. to investigate its potential in new contexts, particularly on the Net), and by the objectives of the Compendium development team to build an open, extensible system to serve as a research platform. Beyond minor extensions, effort has not focused on changing the IBIS formalism, since its value in the field has proven itself to our satisfaction. We have however focused on how to make it more usable, and on the skills required to exploit software-enhanced IBIS, particularly in meeting scenarios (cf. Conklin's work on Dialogue Mapping and Selvin's work on Participatory Hypermedia Construction)."

Compendium is a powerful, fast developing and well supported software. It has developed a significant user base of over 94,800 downloads of the software and over 1750 Compendium Group subscribers and over 140 Compendium Developer Group members. Although free software, it is used by multiple high profile organisations such as: Nasa Ames Research Center, World Trade Organization, UNESCO, Verizon (formerly Bell Atlantic), Touchstone Consulting Group, Pitney Bowes, GlaxoSmithKline, AETMIS (Province of Quebec government agency), LIMSI (France) to support argument visualisation for dealing with complex problems (Sevin, 2006, pers. comm. 16 November; van Hoof et al. 2005). Specifically, within NASA it continues to support the collaborative modelling of work systems (Buckingham Shum et al. 2006). Practical applications of Compendium cited by Sierhuis (2006) from the RIACS/NASA Ames Research Center include: meetings, process modelling, dataflow modelling, decision rationale, teaching and learning content, research, course work, note-taking & study tool, executive roundtable, policy decision-making, distributed collaboration, and communicating analyses.

Additional diagramming software trialled were **Inspiration, ConceptDraw MINDMAP, FreeMind, Athena Standard,** and **Athena Negotiator**. These did not add anything conceptually new nor of value beyond those discussed above and therefore, have not been discussed. An exception might be the Athena products, which are also free products and do have features for weighting nodes and evaluating argumentation but in comparison to Compendium, was deficient in several other areas relevant to this project. These areas were, representation capabilities, importing of external files, argument ontology and node notation, coping with large quantities of data (e.g. hyperlinking) and collaborative operation.

CSAV Software Preference

Compendium met most of the criteria sought of CSAV software in this project. It provides for freeform map layout and has the functionality to automatically arrange maps in top-down or right-to-left format. Argumentation can be manually evaluated via recognition of colour coding in pro (green) and con (red) node backgrounds but there are no features for argument evaluation such as node weighting. It provides the common text formatting features for the expressive representation of content (i.e. font type & size, bolding, Italics, colour and background fill). It provides a range of node linking options based on IBIS inferences and with basic formatting features (i.e. label font size, bolding, italics & colour). It accommodates the importing of external file types and graphics of any file types and from disparate programmes. It enables the reporting of argumentation and the representation of consultation decisions and resolutions via the use of decision nodes. It provides for different forms of publication such as html and jpeg. Jpeg files can be incorporated into most types of publishing applications. The hyperlinking of map nodes enables the building of a series of maps to cope with high volume content. Compendium offers synchronous collaborative capabilities in that exported XML files of maps can be then imported into the Compendium programme used by other users but more work in this area is underway. There are no specific features for node weighting but weight can be user specified and manually included in maps. Out of the CSAV software trialled, Compendium provided the closest fit to the functionality sought for this project and is free software; hence, for this project the value for money criterion is also satisfied.

Conclusion

This article has presented an analysis of and discussion about text analysis and argument visualisation software, and the functionality sought and employed for a particular e-Consultation project. Participatory democracy and e-Democracy have the potential to generate a large volume of textual discourse and investigations into technologies to support discourse analysis and representation are required. Initially, natural language text mining with sentiment analysis functionality was posed for investigation but after substantial exploration, text mining was deemed underdeveloped with regard to the specific functionality sought. The text analysis software applications used were Leximancer and TextAnalyst for semi-automated text analysis, Altlas.ti for fine detailed manual text analysis and TextSTAT for word frequency analysis. This multiple application analysis provided triangulation in the text analysis process.

Computer supported argument visualisation was investigated in this project for the purpose of analysing and graphically representing the SEQ Regional Plan Consultation discourse in diagrammatic form. For argument visualisation, Compendium was the chosen application from among twelve trialled applications. Compendium was found to be well supported with a dynamic development and research community. Compendium provided most of the functionality as deemed relevant to consultation discourse mapping. These consisted of: freeform map structuring, argumentation evaluation, text formatting features, node linking options, the utilisation of disparate file types and ability to report discourse resolutions. It provides for different forms of publication and hyperlinking functionality, has synchronous collaborative capabilities and is an inexpensive programme.

Further Research: An additional part of this project was research conducted on the creation and design of maps created for consultation programmes.

Adrian M, Genovese Y (2011) Analytics and Learning Technology: CIOs, CTOs Should Rethink Art of the Possible.7

Atherton A, Elsmore P (2007) Structuring qualitative enquiry in management and organization research: A dialogue on the merits of using software for qualitative data analysis. Qualitative Research in Organizations and Management 2 (1):15

Bachler M, Buckingham Shum S, Selvin A (2006) Compendium. 1.5.1 Beta 6. 1.5.1 Beta 6 edn. Compendium Institute, Washington DC, US

Bachler M, Prabhakaran L, Contributor: Ehrich S (2007) Compendium. 1.5.2 edn. Open University, Milton Keynes: UK

Baez M, Birukou A, Casati F, Marchese M (2010) Addressing Information Overload in the Scientific Community. IEEE Computer Society NOVEMBER/DECEMBER:31-38

Banxia Software Ltd (2004) Decision Explorer. Standard Edition edn. Banxia Software Ltd, Kendal: UK

Banxia Software Ltd. (2002) Decision Explorer®: Advance Decision Support Software for Ideas Mapping. Banxia Software Ltd. http://www.banxia.com/demain.html. Accessed 8th Febraury 2005

Blismas N, Dainty A (2003) Computer-aided qualitative data analysis: panacea or paradox? Building Research and Information 31 (6):455-463

Bontis N, Fearon M, Hishon M (2003) The e-flow audit: an evaluation of knowledge flow within and outside a high-tech firm. Journal of Knowledge Management 7 (1):6-19

Bringer J, Johnston L, Brackenridge C (2004) Maximising transparency in a doctoral thesis: the complexities of writing about the use of QSR*NVIVO within a grounded theory study. Qualitative Research 4 (2):247-265

Buckingham Shum S, Selvin A, Sierhuis M, Conklin J, Haley C, Nuseibeh B (2006) Hypermedia Support for Argumentation-Based Rationale: 15 Years on from gIBIS and QOC. In: Dutoit A, McCall R, Mistrik I, Paech B (eds) Rationale Management in Software Engineering Springer-Verlag/Computer Science Editorial, pp 111-132

Carenini M, Whyte A, Bertorello L, Vanocchi M (2007) Improving Communication in E-democracy Using Natural Language Processing. Intelligent Systems: IEEE 22 (1):20-27

Centers for Disease Control and Prevention (2003) AnSWR. 6.2.x edn., Atlanta: US

Coleman S, Norris D (2005) A new agenda for e-democracy, A New Agenda for E-democracy: Lessons from Initiatives Round the World. Oxford Internet Institute (OII): Oxford University, Oxford: UK

Conklin J, Basadur M, VanPatter G (2007) Rethinking Wicked Problems: Unpacking Paradigms, Bridging Universes. NextD Journal: ReReThinking Design 10 (10.1):30

Copernic Inc. (2001) Copernic Summarizer. 2.0 edn., Montreal: Canada

Coredge Software Inc. (2003) Logik. My Edition 2.5 edn., Ottawa: Canada

Dainty A, Bagilhole B, Neale R (2000) Computer aided analysis of qualitative data in construction management research. Building Research and Information 28 (4):226-233

De Liddo A, Buckingham Shum S Capturing, Mapping and Integrating Argumentation as Project Memory in Participatory Urban Planning. In: DEMO-net Workshop on Argumentation Support Systems for eParticipation, , Berlin: Germany, March 5, 2007, 2007.

Durian D (2002) Corpus-Based Text Analysis from a Qualitative Perspective: A Closer Look at NVivo. Style 36 (4):738-742

Eden C (1992) On the Nature of Cognitive Maps. Journal of Management Studies 29 (3):261-265

Eppler M, Mengis J (2004) The Concept of Information Overload: A Review of Literature from Organization Science, Accounting, Marketing, MIS, and Related Disciplines. Information Society 20 (5):325-344

Ficco S, Karamychev V (2004) Information Overload in Multi-Stage Selection Procedures. Tinbergen Institute Discussion Paper:1-19

Fouts R, Rozwell C (2011) Marketing Essentials: How to Integrate Social Media Into Your Marketing Communications Strategy.15

Gilbert L (2002) Going the distance: 'closeness' in qualitative data analysis software. International Journal of Social Research Methodology 5 (3):215-228

Huning M (2007) TextStat. 2.7 edn. Free University of Berlin, Berlin: Germany

IBM (2004) DB2 Information Integrator OmniFind Edition. 8.2 edn. IBM, Cambridge: US

Institute for Human and Machine Cognition (2007) CmapTools. 4.09 edn. Institute for Human and Machine Cognition,

Jankowski N, Leeuwis C, Martin P, Noordhof M, Rossum J Teledemocracy in the Province: an Experiment with Internet-based software and Public Debate. In: EURICOM Colloqium, June 1997.

Kirschner P, Buckingham Shum S, Carr CE (2003) Visualizing Argumentation: Software Tools for Collaborative and Educational Sense-Making. Springer, London: UK

Kirshchner P, Buckingham Shum S, Carr CE (2003) Visualizing Argumentation: Software Tools for Collaborative and Educational Sense-Making. Springer, London: UK

Kunz W, Rittel H (1979) Issues as Elements of Information Systems. (Working Paper 131):1-10

Macintosh A Characterizing E-Participation in Policy-Making. In: Proceedings of the 37th Hawaii International Conference on System Sciences, Hawaii, 2004. IEEE, pp 1-10

Macintosh A, Renton A Argument Visualisation to support democratic decision-making. In: eChallenges e.2004 Conference, Vienna, Austria, 27-29 October 2004. p 8

Mack R, Mukherjea S, Soffer A, Uramoto N, Brown E, Coden A, Cooper J, Inokuchi A, Iyer B, Mass Y, Matsuzawa H, Subramaniam L (2004) Text analytics for life science using the Unstructured Information Management Architecture. IBM Systems Journal 43 (3)

Macmillan K, Koenig T (2004) The Wow Factor: Preconceptions and Expectations for Data Analysis Software in Qualitative Research. Social Science Computer Review 22 (2):179-186

Mangabeira W, Lee R, Fielding N (2004) Computers and qualitative research: Adoption, use, and representation. Social Science Computer Review 22 (2):11

McFadden T (2003) Leximancer Version. 2.0 edn. Leximancer Pty Ltd, Brisbane: Australia

MicroSystems Co. Ltd. (2003) TextAnalyst. 2.3 edn., Moscow: Russia

Mindjet LLC (2007) MindManager Pro 6. 6.2.399 edn. Mindjet LLC, San Francisco: US

Morse J, Richards L (2002) Readme First for a User's Guide to Qualitative Methods. Sage, London: UK

Muhr T (2004) Atlas.ti. 5.0 edn. Scientific Software Development., Berlin: Germany

Nasukawa T, Yi J Sentiment Analysis: Capturing Favorability Using Natural Language Processing. In: Second International Conference on Knowledge Capture, Sanibel Island: US, October 23–25 2003. ACM Press,

OECD (2003) Promise and Problems of e-Democracy: Challenges of Online Citizen Engagement. Organisation for Economic Co-operation and Development,

OECD (2004) Promise and Problems of e-Democracy: Challenges of Online Citizen Engagement. OECD,

QSR International Pty Ltd (2002) Nvivo. 2.0 edn. QSR International Pty Ltd, Melbourne: Australia

Rathee R, Rishi R (2011) E-GOVERNANCE: PROMISES AND CHALLENGES. International Journal of Information Technology and Knowledge Management 4 (2):443-445

Reed C, Rowe G (2003) Araucaria. 3.1 edn. University of Dundee, Dundee: UK

Rittel H, Webber M (1984) Planning problems are wicked problems. Developments in Design Methodology. Wiley, New Jersey: US

Shegda K, Chin K, Lundy J, Bell T, Logan D, Eid T (2004) Magic Quadrant for Enterprise Content Management.

Sierhuis M Compendium. In: Computational Semantics Laboratory, Stanford University, Stanford: UK, September 28 2006.

Smith A (2004a) Lexmancer: The Document Mapping System. www.leximancer.com. Accessed 15th December 2004

Smith A (2004b) Leximancer Manual (Version 2.0). in association with the University of Queenland, Queensland: Australia

Smith Aa, Humpreys M (2006) Evaluation of unsupervised semantic mapping of natural language with Leximancer concept mapping. Behavior Research Methods 38 (2):262-279

Soliman J, Kan M Grounded Theory and NVivo: Wars and Wins. In: QualIT2004: International Conference on Qualitative Research in IT & IT in Qualitative Research, Brisbane: Australia, 2004. p 9

Suthers D Collaborative Knowledge Construction through Shared Representations. In: 38th Hawaii International Conference on the System Sciences (HICSS-38), Waikoloa, Hawaii, January 3-6 2005. p pp. 10

Suthers D, Burger D (2002) Belvedere. 4.1 edn. University of Hawaii, Manoa: Hawaii

Swedish Morphological Society (2005) Wicked Problems: Structuring Social Messes with Morphological Analysis. http://www.swemorph.com/wp.html Accessed 6th July 2011

Toulmin S, Rieke R, Janik. A (1984) An introduction to reasoning (2nd ed.). Macmillan., New York: US

Uramoto N, Matsuzawa H, Nagano T, Murakami A, Takeuchi H, Takeda K (2004) A text-mining system for knowledge discovery from biomedical documents. IBM Systems Journal 43 (3):516-533

Van Gelder T, Bulka A (2002) Reasonable. 1.1ca edn. Austhink, Melbourne: Australia

van Hoof R, Zimmermann B, Selvin A, Buckingham Shum S, Cornish H, Bachler M, Sutcliffe S, Mazzeo J (2005) Compendium: Associated Institutions. Compendium Institute. http://compendium.open.ac.uk/institute//institutions.htm. Accessed 12 May 2007

Weitzman E (2003) Software and Qualitative Research. In: Denzin N, Lincoln Y (eds) Collecting and interpreting qualitative materials (2nd ed.). Sage Publications, London: UK,

Welsh E (2002) Dealing with Data: Using NVivo in the Qualitative Data Analysis Process. Forum: Qualitative Social Research 3 (2):7

Whyte A, Macintosh A (2003) Analysis and Evaluation of e-consultation. e-Service Journal 2 (1):9-35

Wigmore J (1931) The Principles of Judicial Proof or the Process of Proof as Given by Logic, Psychology, and General Experience, and Illustrated in Judicial Trials. 2nd edition. Little, Brown and Company,, Boston, MA

Woelfel J (1998) Catpac II. 2.0 edn. The Galileo Company, New York: US